The Rain-Giver

By the same author

The Rain-Giver

Poems by
Kevin Crossley-Holland

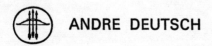

ANDRE DEUTSCH

First published 1972 by
André Deutsch Limited
105 Great Russell Street London WC1

Copyright © 1972 by Kevin Crossley-Holland

Printed in Great Britain by
Clarke Doble & Brendon Ltd
Plymouth

ISBN 0 233 96355 3

Contents

Acknowledgments

Thanks are due and gladly given to the editors of the following publications in which some of these poems first appeared: Agenda, Ambit, Aquarius, The Beloit Poetry Journal, Encounter, The Irish Times, The Listener, The New York Times, Outposts, *PEN Anthologies 1967 and 1970*, Poetry and Audience, The Poetry Review, Priapus, Quarry, Queen, A Review of English Literature, The Spectator, The Sunday Times, The Times Literary Supplement, Tribune, Twentieth Century, Wave, *Young Winter's Tales, The Young British Poets*.

'For My Son', 'The Rain-Giver', 'Your Imitations' and 'My Son' first appeared in *My Son*, published in a limited edition by Turret Books.

Alderney: The Nunnery was first published in a limited edition by Turret Books.

Eight of these poems first appeared in *Norfolk Poems* published in a limited edition by Academy Editions.

'Confessional' and 'A Dream of a Meeting' have been published as leaflets and 'The Island' as a poster by The Sceptre Press.

'Mirror Edged with Shells' has been printed as a poemcard by the Dædalus Press, and as an etching by Eric Malthouse.

Several of these poems have been broadcast on 'Poetry Now', and from BBC East Anglia.

Finally, I must thank the E. C. Gregory Trust and the University of Leeds for appointing me Gregory Fellow in Poetry, 1969–1971.

7

A Dream of a Meeting

Rooted I watch, watch the girl
approach in a street hedged with
poppies, trembling, hollyhocks
nodding their acquiescence.
There are always hollyhocks.
Gravely she walks with perfect
equilibrium; daylight
sleepwalker, ashen-faced,
she looms towards this meeting
she knows nothing of.
                           I strain
my eyes to see her features
as a sculptor searches stone,
finding there correlatives
of his own huge passion.
Her face is a lily spathe
with no blemish, and her hair,
moon-pale, falls out behind her.
Green-sheathed she grows now, grows
towards me.
                    And then I see
she is only eight, maybe
nine. A cigarette, unlit,
waits in her mouth. Still rooted,
I frown like the puritan
I am, I still partly am.
No, not a cigarette, no,
it is a thermometer
jammed under her tongue; the sun
angles off it.
                    And she comes
so very close now, at last
she sees me, hands outstretched.
Her eyes are child's marbles

as she gives me the slender,
gleaming stem of glass, passes
by me; and she does not even
change her metronomic pace.
The sap surges within me,
I look for the mercury :
it is all, all in the bulb,
in the bulb this summer day.
Rooted, I ache. And the girl
goes on gravely. Unknowing,
she brushes trembling poppies
with her bare legs; their scarlet
petals spill like drops of blood.
And all the hollyhocks nod.

Our Love's

A moonstone, Methusalah,
a just-discovered discoverer,
a seventh wave, lump of yeast,
warmonger, advocate of peace,
an unknown quantity, partly guile,
pardoner – pockets crammed with smiles,
a rock pool, embryo growing,
breakable, our lives' poem,
Joseph's flower, much more, in a jot.
Our love is when words are not.

Epithalamium

for Stephen and Judy Kane

The sun struck at you where you stood,
still separate, and braced bright bands
around you. It was momentary,
but absolute; then you moved on,
and in your train bridesmaid and page
uncompromised.
           All down the nave
the congregation, topped and tailed,
was mottled in the light stained glass
had caught, and altered, and passed on;
blotched red and yellow, blue, green, they
sneaked glances at each other, sang
together, watched the bride and groom.

Watched and identified: for one
a dream, and one a dream gone wrong,
for one never to come, and one
not even now a dream; and then,
through you, some sense renewed of all
that's possible, always being
unfulfilled.
          That hot Saturday
in June in a dormitory town,
the purpose of a pilgrimage:
we gazed at your coincidence,
that where you stood, by some good chance
light fell unstained and married you.

Suggestions

The convoluted exercise begins:
A shooting star from some galactic seam

Gravitated, flaring, a scream of light
Arrowing to its soft grave, this planet.

Or else, it was as if he were a star
Shot, breathless, down the gallery of air.

Or, he was some meteor from heaven
Burning and always falling, since Adam.

By symbol, simile and metaphor
I hide the nakedness of the idea.

Suggestion makes the dream, said Mallarmé.
Would I deny the poem if I denied

This first, second, and third remove, excised
The convolutions, *called* it making love?

Pregnancy

You sleep so fitfully, skittering
over deep waters; waking, you will crave
sleep.
      The air trembles with dreams.

The flutter of bird from bough
no longer quickens you, stars do not quiet
you.
      Eighth month, my love; nearly dawn.

For My Son

I wish him to be master of the gong.
Who, striking it, will release the song
Of all tones in one harmony. He will not be.
Yet, let his apprenticeship be lifelong,
Let him at least distinguish right from wrong
And hear, sometimes, the freedom of that mastery.

My Son: Five Poems

1

This is the most terrible thing: his world
Excludes me. What is not darkened by this?
I am admitted to his presence, hurled
In with imprecations, with that snake's hiss

That I do not love him, do not love him
Who is my son. He stumbles through my dreams.
His mother, though, is gentle, and lacking
In that other's sting. She will quiet his screams.

What is there? My heart and left hand falter.
The grass withers under my tread, the leaf
Darkens on the tree. His eyes did not alter
At my coming. What will exorcise this grief?

Late and drenched I came. The skies did not bless
That visit to my son. I hurried in,
Half my allotted time already run,
Keyed up too long for this occasion.
She welcomed me with that familiar smile,
Unhurried, partly sad. How could I smile
At her whom I betrayed? And yet I felt
Aggrieved to be, so late, longer delayed.

And then I was shown in. Oh he was there,
Not expecting me, nor yet especially
Pleased that I had come. The door clicked shut
On us, left ostentatiously alone.
Cautiously we grinned, moved round each other
Wary as boxers; then dropped to the floor
And there, his pile of bricks dividing us,
Once more began to reconstruct the walls.

'Peter. Time for bed.' I did not hear her
Enter. He understood, looked at the walls,
At me; and, as he used to do, lurched
Forward, propped himself against my knee.
Oh then I knew all I had lost for ever:
When he believed I could afford him
Sanctuary, my paper smiles tore, the walls
We built together first tottered, then fell.

3

'I insist.' And with both fists I banged
The table-top. 'Is it unreasonable,
This one request that I should see my son?'
All reason ended then. I damned myself.
My error was to be so adamant.

An hour or more we quarrelled over him
Before I saw the thing's futility.
So I gave in, gave half my life to end
Such bitterness. For neither could afford
Its cost. Where both had hoped to win, both lost.

That night, such storms. O God, storms such as I
Have never known. Love, hate and deep remorse
Grappled within me all night long. I lay torn
Beyond tears; and then, spent by such anguish,
Silent in the utter loneliness of dawn.

Three months apart we had agreed upon;
But when I called to see her one last time,
Repentant she began : 'I do not want to seem
Unfair. And yes, he needs a father's hand.
Why not come once a week as we first planned?'

I walked away on waves of air, giddy
At her revocation. And for some time
That night went out of mind. Clearly I saw
There are at times irreconcilables
When both can win if one will first withdraw.

4

At other times there was little enough
That showed. Once she saw me at the corner
Of the road, quickened her step towards me.

We spoke few words and those were pleasantries.
There was a certain tenderness, the refusal
At last to hurt where we could avoid it.

She wore a simple, cotton frock that day
That swayed to her quick steps as she led me
To where he played, sitting cross-legged, alone,

A Buddha in his sanctuary. A moment
She stayed, but then withdrew; she knew
Her presence would lay claim to his affection.

And afterwards it was almost the same.
I left him in his room, dropping asleep,
And went as quietly as I had come.

Only then such heaviness clamped round my heart.
I saw once more the failure we had made,
And sensed the loss that each tried now to hide.

As it was once. . . . But was it ever so?
Such tares take root and grow in their own time;
They lay there always, sleeping through our spring.
And yet my son. . . . From this flawed thing we made,
He came. He is unbruised. And I so long
For all his childhood to be so, I say
'As it was once', and dream nothing is wrong
That I cannot repair, all I need do
Assemble my belongings and return.

The Rain-Giver

A two-year-old boy gazes up at a glass cupola, the outside of which his father is washing. Later, both father and son stare up at the cupola together.

DAY

The sky's visor opened: there was a face,
Immense and undefined, bearing down on you
Who staggered round the stairhead, dangerously,
Looking up at the glass, and through the glass,
At the clouds crossing. And you were awed
As the face dissolved in water streams,
Then reformed, better defined, still blurred
By the uneven, eighteenth-century glass.
This I saw, precarious on the cracking slates,
Bucket in hand, cleaning the cupola.
And you called out, a loud, demanding shout,
Perhaps to cover your uncertainty.
You shrank when I replied with reassurances;
My disembodied call reverberated
Down the flights, died shivering in the hall.

NIGHT

There was thunder, somewhere, a long way off
And never nearer, like a gong struck lightly.
Dusk came; you could hear it no longer,
And the rain came, softly – a shadow stealing up
Then rapping at the cupola. 'Rain,'
You called, 'rainrain.' We stood on the stairhead,
Peering into the black, topless hole.
You know he lives there, though you cannot see him.

He hides from you behind a mask of darkness,
The powerful one, the rain-giver. He stands
Behind the panes and smacks them with his hands;
You laugh and acknowledge him again and again.
And now you call out for my attention,
Point out the dark stain which has seeped
Through the cupola, trickles down the wall.

Sober as a Judge

The court sits; you hold it.
But you'll never make a judge,
My only son, drunk in charge.
What is your capacity?

My clown and your own,
You reel about all day,
Laughing or crying
Without any subtlety.
How slight the distinction;
You change masks abruptly.
Sleep fells you at seven;
The lines settle then. I rise
And read the inheritance
From which I can't protect you.

Come on then, my drunkard,
My small son. The court waits
To judge you. I dare you :
Walk here without a fall.

Your Imitations

Your imitations gratify, your endless intimations
Of a tie you take for granted and cannot think to question.
All afternoon you've trailed me and sucked my pipe the wrong
    way up,
(Beware of that, beware at Halloween!). Your teeth, new and
    sharp,
Grip the stem as fiercely as a ferret at the neck of rat
Or rabbit. These animals, all three, you've left at the back
Of the cupboard in the nursery. No toys fascinate you
As mine do. You're forever switching switches, smeared with
    glue,
Opening and shutting books each one of which is closed to you.
I look at the clock; and so do you, heavy-lidded, hectic,
Avoiding my eye. Our blood-knot tightens at these intimations.
Must I deny you sleep, or myself these imitations?

A Dream and a Death

Your Imitations

He had died in his sleep. Who sleep had taken
by surprise, not insidiously inching up
from behind, but with the clean blow of an axe.
It felled him like the sapling he was.
He had been listening to the great wind outside
wrenching at the roots, battering the rib-cage
of the old elm. Listening and thinking:
improbable, human tree, more likely
to succumb to the onslaught of a bumble bee.

Relatives and friends had gathered round his bed,
not at all surprised. He would have liked to know
what they said who gazed so openly at him;
but being dead, he did not know. Like shoals
of aimless leaves they scraped about, not distraught
yet not prepared to go, severing
the link for ever. And there were many things
he had wanted to say (or, more precisely,
would have wanted to say), and could not now.

His eyes opened: the room was empty
and shuddering, and the curtains beat like wings.
He walked to the window and looked down
from a great height. He saw it lying there,
stunned and helpless, so astoundingly green,
still breathing. People were already
gathering around it out of curiosity;
they stared at it and fingered it;
the wind still moaned in it. He turned away,
passionate and constricted, as if he was dreaming.

Gun Hill Revisited

Part II

BEWARE, it said, in red capitals,
WHEN THE RED FLAG IS FLYING;
but the salted wind had eaten away
the reason, and there was no flagstaff now.
I knew, I remembered it
as soon as I saw that tilted board,
standing on one leg, a dune-crest from the sea.
I gave my wife three guesses:
her first, 'Beware of the tides';
her second, 'Beware of the Shuck';
her last, 'Beware of the Red Flag'.
I told her then of how, a boy,
sudden rabbits startling me, marram grass prickling,
I hunted for spent cartridges,
burnished crayons half-bedded in dunes.
(What afternoons!) I hoarded them
in my pockets, made holsters of my socks;
and later I stacked them
in my grandfather's spent cigar box.
I remember the coils of barbed wire,
the concrete emplacements I never questioned
and no one cared to explain.
It is as if they had never been.
There is only this board, ambiguous,
that I must have seen before,
emblem both of happiness and war.

The Shuck is a huge dog, either headless or with eyes like saucers, that prowls along the Norfolk coast by night.

The Wall

I am a desolate wall, accumulator of lichen.
Men made me with flint chippings and, fickle as always,
ignored me; time did not ignore them.
My business is to divide things : the green ribbons
of grass from the streams of macadam; the kitchen gardens
from the marsh acres, garish with sea-lavender;
the copses of ilex and pine from the North Sea,
the bludgeoning waves of salt water where seabirds play.
I stand grey under the East Anglian sky,
glint when the occasional sun opens its eye.

My business is to divide things, my duty to protect.
I am unrepaired; men neglect me at their own risk.
Time takes me in mouthfuls; the teeth of the frost
bit into my body here; here my mortar crumbles;
the wind rubs salt into every wound.
Elsewhere I am overgrown with insidious ivy;
it wound its arms around me only to strangle me.

Relentless, the sea rolls down from the Pole.
It levelled the dunes last year, removed the marram grass,
clashed its steel cymbals over marsh and macadam.
It attacked me and undermined me; I sway
like a drunkard now; yet it could not gash me
with its gleaming scythes; it was not strong enough.
I stand, sad, and stare at all this estate,
the lawns, the kitchen gardens, copses garrulous
in the wind. I carefully listen, listen and wait
for the fierce outsider to force his way in.

Advent Lyric

translated from Old English

. . . . to the King.
You are the corner-stone the builders
once discarded. It becomes you well
to stand at the head of the great hall,
to lock together the lengthy walls,
the unbreakable flint, in your firm embrace,
so that all things on earth with eyes
may marvel endlessly at the Lord of Grace.
O true-battle-bright One, reveal now your own might
through your mysterious skill, but let wall
still remain upright against wall. The hall needs
the care of the Craftsman, and the King Himself,
that he should repair and restore the ruined house
under its roof. He created the body's limbs
of clay. Now the Lord of Life must save
rejected men from devils, deliver the wretched
from damnation, as He has often done before.

Spring Tide, Burnham-Overy-Staithe

Sea undermines the sand-cliffs,
unties marram knots.

Surges of dark water
sweep sand into the creeks

patrolled by pirate skuas.
Shrikes and kittiwakes

fly in with the flood,
driven from their drift-nests

on Scolt Head. The groynes,
channels, side-gullies

cannot contain this tide;
white sea-stallions

race over the saltmarsh,
thrift and thistle and mud.

Waves lap, and slap
the base of Burnham dyke

that frowns, unforgetful
of the great flood. Gorse

half-hides its scars – sandbags
cement blocks, giant spars.

Bitterns boom their warning
now as the water rises.

Men shoal on the Staithe.

Dusk, Burnham-Overy-Staithe

The blue hour ends, this world
floats on a great stillness.

I only guess where marsh
finishes and sky begins,

each grows out of the other.
In the creek a slip

of water gleams. Rowboats
bob and swing above the mud,

the barnacled and broken
ribs of Old Stoker's boat.

A wedge of gulls rustles
overhead, and for a moment

the water notices them.
Such calm is some prelude.

Then across the marsh it comes,
the sound as of an endless

train in a distant cutting,
the god working his way back,

butting and shunting,
reclaiming his territory.

This world's his soundbox now;
in the stillness he still moves.

Anything could happen.

A Beach of Stones

That stadium of roaring stones,
The suffering. O they are not dumb things,
Though bleached and worn, when water
Strikes at them. Stones will be the last ones;
They are earth's bones, no easy prey
For breakers. And they are not broken
But diminish only, under the pestle,
Under protest. They shift through centuries,
Grinding their way towards silence.

c

Marshland

This green land is almost inviolate.
Men have come, regarding it
As some commodity;
It will throw them off its outraged back.
Look at the surrendered houses,
The houseboats that will be next year's wrack.
Nothing changes.
As surely as the Black Death
Ribbed the sodden fields with graves,
And stranded churches like whales,
The marsh vapours
Rise and will drive intruders off.

Those who commune with this green land,
As their fathers did,
Intend no change, only survival.
They walk like penitents
Behind herds of lean cattle,
Salt-savaged ploughshares.
They talk of rot and marsh tares
And their horizons are dykes
Before the distant changes of the sea.
They are tight with few harvests,
Little loving;
In their damp bones they know belonging.

Geese

At the skim of evening
Wild geese fly inland

Then immense silence
Sends most men to their houses

Confessional

I come once more to this terrible place;
As it was it is, each stone and each face

Unchanged, making an index of the change
In me. Everything here was arranged

Long ago; the wind, raking from the north,
Saw to that and sees to it. In the hearth

Coals glow and the ash flies early and late;
Every face is ruckled, sands corrugate;

Inland, those superstitious hawthorn trees
Strain away from the wind and heckled seas.

Yet I come. Here alone I cannot sham.
The place insists that I know who I am.

Elemental trinity – earth, air, sea –
Harshly advocate my humility:

You are bigoted, over-ambitious,
You are proud, you salute the meretricious.

Then I have altered this much with the years:
That I need more to admit my errors,

From fear, and a longing not to be blind;
So I am scoured by the unchanging wind,

And rid again of some superfluity
By that force uninterested in me.

And I can go, prepared for the possible;
Dream and bone set out from the confessional.

The Frisian Wife

translated from the Old English Gnomic Verses

Frost will forge fetters, fire devour timber,
Earth will quicken and ice build crystal bridges;
Water will be straight-jacketed, will shackle
Reeds and sprouting seeds. But one shall put asunder
The fetters of frost – most mighty God.
Winter will melt, fair weather will return,
Summer, the scorching sun. The waters are restless then.
. . . . Dear is the welcome one
To the Frisian wife when the ship sails in;
His boat is berthed, her own husband is back,
The man who maintains her, and she leads him home.
She washes his salt-stained garments and gives him clean clothing;
She grants him on land all that he, her lover, asks.
A wife must observe her marriage oath; women are often deceivers.
If one is faithful, the next is fickle,
Harbouring strangers while her husband is over the sea.
His voyage is long but the sailor will wait for his loved one,
Wait for all he cannot hurry for. And then, at last,
Unless he is sick or the sea stays him, he sails home.
The sea holds him in her hands. . . . . . .

Mirror Edged with Shells

Sea-things, in colours of the sea
that might not match, and do : jade-green, grey-green,
sallow, foam, indigo. They are accustomed
to perpetual movement, the emery
of sandgrains shifting to and fro,
water's infinite progressions and recessions.
They lack lustre now they are quite motionless,
these scaled, brittle protectors, framing
the still water of the glass which reflects them.

Which reflects you too, beautiful
now only that, looking, you see
all weathers in your face. Until the water
moves at last with you, clear and unfathomable;
the quiet shells, at their stations, begin to gleam. . . .

Night-Watchman

No sheet covers her,
The way she lies is foetal.
And her sons sleep
Each in his own darkening room,
Their hands are thrown back above their heads,
Damp finger-twigs twitching, curled.
The watchman waits in the gloom
For the violation
He knows will not come.
From chime to chime
He sits by the wide window,
Husband and father
Still moved by this charge beyond his skills.

Painting by Francis Souza

The smiling skin cannot conceal
The skeleton.
The white skull grins,
Grotesque brain-cage
In which lurk all world-gloom and damage.
Blood-bright flowers rampage around him.

Francis,
Your image of monster-man
Shrithes through my regular room.
He is your 'gentleman of our times',
At a window.
Memento.

The Witness

Your punishment, they said, will be to watch.
We need you as a witness since others
Have witnessed against you. We have built you
A box.
         Then the first walked out of shadows,
Laughing, a sunlight-shaft flanked by ravens;
And when he climbed the wooden steps, as if
To an attic or off on some outing,
He half-turned, hesitant, one hand waving.
The hangman was waiting.
                 Witness, they said,
Count them all once living and now dead.
We are counting on you.
             All afternoon
In that brilliant courtyard I watched them
Come and go, their quick bright faces crossing
From shadow to shadow.
              Keep the tally,
They said.
        But there were only two, it was
A small boy and his brother the hangman
Smothered and smothered and. . . .
              You must not
Turn your eyes. We need you as a witness.
Keep watch, they said.
           But the same two brothers,
There were no others. I know their mother.
Sons flaxen, laughing, still unsuspecting
As I stood and shouted, waved and shouted
Warnings; wept.
         You are free, now go, they said.

Dog-Days

Recovering

Dog-days within the brain

A shell
Put to my own ear
I hear the roaring of blood

This is the septic sign

A rush of air precedes
Cloud-shadows
I speak to them through gauze

The threat and yet no rain

A glass ringing
If I close my eyes
I echo and see smithereens of light

The star must fall in time

Recovering

I am recovering; the quickening sun,
the impatient tendrils seem recoveries.
I dream each spring of being one, and,
dreaming, heal sufficiently.
                                        The grass
thickens, blades grow strong; for a season
only there is nothing but the singing
and the song.
                        Year turns: I shield my eyes
from the sun, lose the lark ascending;
air takes apart its song.
                                    Turning years . . .
each fractures me; and each year I am less
refractory, more hungry for the spring
when I walk in the garden, almost one,
and know I am recovering from being born.

An Old Woman

for George Mackay Brown

Sunday,
she dogs through swerving wind
towards the tolling bell; the swarm
of bees has left that bleached tower.
His blood still quickens hers.

Monday,
no welcome visitors. A rat
scuttles across the courtyard
into her mind. She airs the spare beds.
Nothing is unexpected.

Tuesday,
her aches become flocculent
under hazy sun. She drifts
along the almost empty creek,
and sends to her great-grandson.

Wednesday,
she catches the bus to market.
The eyes of all those young men
make her feel quite skittish.
She dusts her husband's photograph.

Thursday,
on his way to the shop
Old Judson drops in. She humours him
with tea and small orders;
escapes to caulk the scraped keel.

Friday,
earth clings to her bones.
Hectored by winds, her garden
is a rare customary wonder,
her coat of changing colours.

Saturday,
a rumpled sky, wild geese
flying low, threshing huge pinions.
She still stands at the window
long after they are gone.

Going

I am under the auctioneer's hammer,
Going always, never quite gone.
I have been prepared through the summer
And wait as the leaves fall down.

I am the body that survives its song,
No longer bitten by memory or fear
But numb, numb with this always going.
Let me go now I don't care.

After a Medieval Lyric

This hurrying world wheels by;
One man may come, another goes.
What lay ahead lies behind.
All's black that was *couleur de rose*.

Three Sons

The first went shooting and did not come back.
Ravens eclipsed him, strutted on stained ice
And the woman sobbed as she shouldered wrack.

Waves kissed the next, then hurled him against gneiss.
Gold words, ceremony. She stemmed the red
Tide and hugged his duty, his sacrifice.

Stars in his eyes, sudden storms in his head,
The third's the darling joker in the pack.
Everything happens in threes, the woman said.

D

Part IV

Lost and Found

Pickled one night, (as we may surmise from his reputation),
He fell down the well. His disappearance caused a sensation.
Only now has he been found, in the course of excavation:
An old archaeologist in a rare state of preservation.

Stone

If stone should split. . . .

Listen to Sleipnir going like the wind,
Straining sinews on a journey between worlds.
Listen to swords clashing in the flames,
Flashing blades tempered by Weland.
Listen to water, wave after wave
Of laughter, grief breaking in Midgard.

If stone should split. . . .

It is inexorable, older than all things,
Charged with memories, chased with patterns;
It is the eye of the world-hurricane,
Witness of what struggles with time.
Listen! The splitting of stone signifies
One thing: Ragnarok, eruption of aeons.

A Lindisfarne Tombstone

for Eric Elstob

1

Norsemen storm the cells:

The hive ablaze; sluice of blood,
Garnet-bright, under sword and axe;
The golden comb iron reaps;
A knot of monks drone Pax Pax
By candles' light; wax weeps.

A furore Normanorum, libera nos, Domine.

2

Two monks crooked in prayer:

Cuthbert incorrupt and unscathed;
A good haul from Bee Hill;
Quick requital for slaughter;
Freedom from shadows still
Shrithing over the minds' water.

A furore Normanorum, libera nos, Domine.

Celtic monks brought to Lindisfarne the beehive cell; in much Anglo-Saxon jewellery garnets are set in cells of gold.

Mr Kilvert Reflects on the Quarterly Dances

Here we held the Quarterly Dances.
What fun.... What laughing, flirting,
joking and kissing behind the door
or in the dark garden.
                    Home of the winds....
How is all changed, song and dance still,
mirth fled away, only the weird sighing
through the broken roof and crazy doors.
Home of the winds, no longer is the harp
plucked....
            The quick feet, busy hands,
saucy eyes, strong limbs
all mouldered into dust,
the laughing voices silent.
No longer is the harp plucked, no longer
is there happiness in that place.

Alderney: The Nunnery

for Diana and Stephen Mellor

*The oldest building in the Channel Islands, the Nunnery is a
strange mixture of Roman walls and arches, 18th-century
Cotswold manor and German gun emplacements and bunkers.
Although it has known many military occupations, Alderney is
traditionally known as the Island of Rest; it was probably a
cemetery for the inhabitants of the Cotentin peninsula. The
Nunnery today, in peace, embodies this paradox.*

THE ROMANS

Q. Marcius Severus to Antonia in Mediolanum :

You can hold this island in one hand
and a jug of wine in the other.
A settlement huddles at the western end :
fishermen and shepherds whom we do not bother
and who welcomed me ashore with tokens
of esteem.
       I saw today a ring
of 'magic' stones, still unbroken,
where at sundown the people sing
dirges – or so at least they seemed,
so dark and full of droning –
but I am unable to tell you their meaning.
This circle is a gleaming core of light
in the dusk.
       There are no buildings of stone,
only wood, despite much good red granite
which we have used freely for this garrison.
It will house two hundred : a modicum,
you will say. Just so, in comparison
with my headquarters at Constantia.

Nevertheless, it will be adequate
for its purpose.
                    But nest of sea birds,
shags and terns and gannets, rafts
of puffins; haunt of kestrels;
meeting place of easy airs that drift around
with nothing to do, waft to the nostrils
scent of a thousand stamens;
a jar of soporific poppy seeds;
such, Antonia, is this Orniacum.
It is a Greek isle of the Northern seas.
And yet this island is a sword,
a finger length of land flashing under the sun.
we do well to hold it.
                    The billowing
blue hills of Gaul may easily be seen
from this garrison which sits, squat like a toad,
in Longinus Bay, the isle's south-eastern corner.
Away to the left are the sea-roads
to Britain. Our fleet will patrol them.
Word will have reached you of turmoil
in that country – Picts and Scots once more
in the north, Franks and Saxon pirates
sacking southern towns. I fear for Britain,
wraithlike land always slipping from our grasp.
Theodosius will doubtless save it for us
(he is shrewd, that man, and he is ambitious),
And Claudian doubtless find verses
in his honour. Good luck
to Theodosius. But tide after tide
undermines us there. What if the rock
should topple? Tell me, where then will
the landslide stop?
                    These are not disloyal thoughts;
no-one loves Valentinian better than I.
We will scour the channel, chase and sink
each Saxon boat that noses through the sea.
Do not doubt that, Antonia.
                    Behind the reef-shield
and the rock of Raz our fleet lies in wait.

As P. Virgilius Maro wrote :
ancora de prora iacitur; stant litore puppes.

Tomorrow, I return to Constantia.

THE GERMANS

Aurigny, île de silence, de cauchemar
et de l'épouvante. . . .

I saw them I the shepherd Tom Creron
bury men in sacks on Longy Common.
I hid behind a red rock and watched them
file out from the old Nunnery, the wardens
of that storehouse of corpses; I saw them,
every man reeling under the burden
of his own guilt. Many times at sundown
they dug shallow trenches by the dewpond.

Aurigny, île de silence. . . .

I watched them and counted I Tom Creron
just as each evening I count my sheep :
three hundred and seventy-nine Russian men
were slung into those graves – a mass escape.
I lie on my bed and count dead men
and will never sleep. I see it all again;
my dark blood bangs within me; there is no
escape. God forgive them. God forgive them.

Aurigny, île de silence. . . .

The Nunnery takes refuge in her own
growing shadows. Memories are protections.
The sea's wash decorates the vast Roman
walls with an age-old, wavy pattern.
Men brought concrete and corrugated iron
under the arches of that garrison.

58

Earth will stop the bunkers. I Tom Creron
hear now only the flight of the heron

over this island, out of silence,
returning to silence. . . .

THE ISLAND OF REST

Alderney, the eye of the hurricane. Gannets lean into the light
airs. In their scabbards, the pale green swords of grass barely stir.
There has been silence always, many times broken. But silence.

The island contemplates.

Sun glints on the barbed seas. Hints of steel on steel. The Swinge,
The Race of Alderney. The vortex whirls continually. It is
divided in itself. It drags in, until there is no outside, no outsider.

Water spilling over rock, being thrown back. That is how it has
been. Small infringements, endless recessions.

The seventh wave has withdrawn now. The shores and cliffs are
littered with old strategies. Ebb and flow, ebb and flow of water
always moving, so always trapped.

Time and movement pierce the circle ceaselessly. The riots are
not of flowers only. The cries come from children playing soldiers
in the Nunnery.

Island. Centre, not moving in itself, sometimes moved. This is its
sword. It is an inturned eye, released into its own silences.

The Island

Seven days, seven nights in a place of stone:
Atlantic anvil where winds and water hone
Men to what they are, long bundles of bone.

Seven days, seven nights in a place of stone
Where each man learns he is at last alone,
So quickly comes to love, forgive, condone.

Seven days, seven nights in a place of stone.
Saffron flowers in the fissures are soon grown
To all they can become: each one its own

Spirit's song, momentary wild laughter thrown
Against grey walls, the grey sky, the grey sea.

A Plea

This is the time to reduce the volume.
Listen. You can still just walk
In the diminishing peaceable-enough copse
Through green light, amongst under-surfaces.

It is time to do this. Take the leaf
A singular oblique sunshaft lit
And come back listening for difference.
Sound not the screams but each distress.

And the parched ground shall become a pool, and the thirsty land springs of water: in the habitation of dragons, where each lay, shall be grass with reeds and rushes.

ISAIAH